I0418468

Flirting With Freud

Flirting With Freud

A. Skoda

Copyright © 2025 by A. Skoda

All rights reserved. No part of this book may be reproduced in any manner whatsoever without written permission in the case of brief quotations embodied in critical articles and reviews.

First Printing, 2025

Forward

Sigmund Freud is the famed forefather of psychology. His theories focused on the subconscious and how it is revealed through behavior. Freud was adamant that he understood the psychological afflictions women faced. Before him, the only diagnosis women could receive was Hysteria. Despite some advances in psychology, Freud assumed women were driven by sexual needs and functions. This led him to suggest that the lack of a penis resulted in the mental illness he termed Penis Envy.

This illness was thought to be brought on by a subconscious awareness or feeling of castration, that something was missing from a woman due to her physiological differences from men. He assumed this feeling caused most "abnormal" behavior women displayed. With widespread public acceptance of this evaluation, understanding the psychology of women remained stunted as psychologists did not feel the need to pursue further investigation.

Slowly, modern psychologists have begun to debunk this ideology. However, the damage has been done and it will take many more decades to catch up. This is largely due to women being a minority in clinical trials for both mental and physical studies. Clinics are only required to ensure 20% of the test subjects are women- even in trials for women specific research such as birth control and postpartum evaluations. This leads to a wide gap in the true understanding of how women's brains and body's function.

Due to the lack of understanding for their mental and physical health, women have been turning to literature to tell their stories. Yet, their voices are still wildly misunderstood and overlooked.

Be Polite

I don't want to be known

As the girl

With the smile,

The one who waves,

The one who nods politely,

Quietly submitting.

Missing

Missing things

That were never mine

Like the fire

That fuels dreams,

Warmth in the eyes,

Or even something simple,

Like a mind

Not fighting a silent war.

Whispers

Not all things are heard,

But the distinct sounds

Of conflicting voices

Echo within the chambers

Of my skull.

They remind me

I'm teetering

Between the breath of life

And the comfort of death.

They remind me

To look both ways

Before thinking.

They remind me

I'm mortal

That this world will move on without me.

Medicine

She offers me

Different formulas

To help scaffold the discrepancies

Happening inside this mind.

But what does she know?

What does anyone know

About the woman's body?

We aren't studied.

We aren't valued.

Plus, the side effects

Might give death my number,

Let it know where to linger.

Would I surrender?

Journals

Words

Are no longer private

As they seep from

My wrists,

Saturating the paper.

They now belong

To the paper that was supposed

To collect

Every tear, fear, and moment of the day—

For you to analyze.

But for now,

The vibrant stains

Remind me

That someone was there,

Someone could feel—

Whether it be joy or pain.

They remind me

That I am alive,

No matter how they are contorted

When they reach your eyes.

Unavailable

Sullen answers

For unasked questions,

Leading me astray

From the path.

Holding my hand,

Refusing to let go,

You lead me down the road

To a false sense of recovery.

Oedipus

Hard,

Dry,

Humping at 2 pm.

Kissing

Leading to insatiable gasping.

Fondling,

Turning into grasping

Fistfuls of intimacy,

Quenching

A thirst

To feel you,

To taste you,

To hunt down

Every inch of skin.

Fury

Burning bridges

Isn't always bad.

Sometimes,

You need a reminder

To never

Go back.

Prism

Bent,

Refracted

Into what

They call broken

Until my beautiful

Cracks within

Turn into exploited

streams of

Reds,

Yellows,

Greens.

Tightrope

Walking on the tightrope

The chemicals in my brain created,

Linking themselves together,

Knowing I could fall at any moment.

Eyes closed,

Breath held tight,

I pray for balance.

Precariously,

Putting one

Foot

In front of

The other,

Taunted by the murky sea below.

Will I fall in the water?

Will I fall in the sand laced with glass?

Can I trust your hand

To catch me?

Racing Thoughts

Turbulent whirlwinds in my mind.

You took up

The blank spaces

I purposely created,

Blotting ink,

Staining every thought.

You strung words

So eloquently

Around my heart,

Unable to let go

And let me be.

Stability

The rocks under my feet

Become loose without warning.

My strong stance, once again,

Becomes tumultuous

As I try to gain stability.

My feet losing grip

Forces my eyes to stare over the cliff

I am bound to slip off

Into the darkness.

The eerie promise of nothingness,

The fear of falling replaced quickly

By the fear of never touching the ground again.

Deep night encompassing me

I'm Alice, falling down the rabbit hole.

Silently screaming for

Someone,

Anyone,

To catch me.

But the white rabbit never comes.

Nobody does.

Nobody can hear me.

My grin is plastered too well onto my face.

You are distracted,

And cannot see as I slip

Off

The

Cliff.

We Don't

We don't know

Love.

We know

When boys think we're:

Pretty,

Beautiful,

Sexy,

Cute,

Desirable,

Sensational,

Fuckable.

Why We Don't Talk

I like my doors closed

Away from the bright lights,

Away from the noise,

Away from the tiresome phrases.

Because really,

How do I do?

Does that even interest you?

This way, my thoughts are still my own,

Untangled,

Unknotted,

Unafraid of being told something about myself

I already know.

Depression

Swallowed up

In your sweet saliva,

I could never quite find

My place

Until you digested me.

Empty,

Depleted,

Without grace.

Self-Medicating

Am I ready to do this

Dip my toes in your waters,

Deep with:

Wine, whiskey, vodka,

Weed, Xanax, Valium,

Opioids, heroin.

How far will I wade

Into your promising light,

Into your promising eyes,

Thinking it will be alright,

Before I must hold my breath,

Just hoping to survive?

Endless Tunnels

Unsure of when the tunnel began,

I step lightly, waving my torch,

Hoping to find daylight.

The must and moss grow

As dopamine leaves my body

With each step I take.

You said there would be light.

You said there would be a silver lining.

But no matter the pills I pop,

The talks I give,

The endless naps and sleepless nights

Light still cannot reach me.

Intellect

My heart yearns

For an intellectual rendezvous

The kind that spits words,

Igniting my blood.

Enticing words that stare me down,

Bringing comfort to the fire

Deep within my soul.

Stringing thoughts together,

Steady as a stream.

Being taken seriously

A rare delight.

Silent Symptoms

My words flip and flop

Between my teeth,

Drip off the tip of my tongue

Humming anxiously,

Between my twiddling thumbs.

They vanish before they even exist,

Slipping from thought to breath,

Into nonexistence.

When Asked to Speak

Sticky, mushy

Sentences

Forced through gritted teeth,

Mulled around by

Aspirated aspirations.

You're Cute When You're Mad

Anger is cute

When it's bursting from a woman

Less than 5'3.

Her stature small,

Her frame soft,

Her looks betray.

Stubbornness is mocked

Because how could a woman

Truly stand her ground

With the stares of men pressing her down?

Passionate dissonance

Must simply be PMS.

"It's a month-long cycle, you know."

Feelings are discarded

Across the freeway,

Lying helplessly,

Like a lost shoe.

Tangled with the emotional garbage

Toxic masculinity

Refuses to see.

Kintsugi

My laughter,

If loud enough,

Permeates through the heartbreak.

My laughter, if loud enough,

Will deceive my heart.

It will flourish

Inside my soul

And allow

The broken parts

To seal themselves with gold.

Blame

Blame me for being

What I was bred to be

Spreading my legs,

My mouth,

My body,

Only to be immersed in

tangled expectations.

You will never know the haunting

Echoes and memories

I have to relive

Every time

You measure my worth,

My love,

By my willingness to accept

Your girth.

But go ahead

Blame me.

Call It a Tantrum (I Dare You)

Slamming doors,

Tears erode my face

Into rivers,

Canyons

Filled with disgrace.

Screams echo for miles.

Why does it have to be this way?

Control lost once more,

Fleeing through the first

Open door.

Crowns

Awaiting the day

A crown of dignity

Can be placed upon my head

The scepter of virtue in hand,

Replacing the jester's suit

That betrayed me.

Spitfire

Yeah, I stand taller

Just to make the world a little smaller.

They say

I'm resilient, they say I'm strong

As if I had a choice.

To climb higher than the rest,

To stand taller than any of them,

I had to.

Fight

Because of my stature, my gender,

The time I became

A mother.

I must fight constantly:

For my voice

To be heard above the roar of the crowds,

For my needs to be met,

Because society demands a woman be everything

A mother, an employee, a wife, a sibling, a daughter.

Yet I have passions, wishes, and dreams,

And I'll be damned if society decides

None of these can come to fruition

Simply because I harbor responsibilities

Bigger than me.

Because my voice is soft,

Because I'm only 5'1.

So yeah,

I stand taller.

They call me a spitfire, hysterical

But it was out of necessity,

So, I wouldn't get written off

Like the women before me.

Victim

I'm not a victim, but

I've been victimized.

Victimized by a society

That taught young boys and girls

Consent is a social nicety,

Like saying thank you,

Like kindness is expected.

Victimized by antiquated ideas

That a woman's body is still a man's property,

That dissent only goes so far

Before affection is demanded.

Victimized by the idea that rejection

Might be a sign of admiration.

A game of cat and mouse never interested me.

Victimized by the notion that my body is a battleground,

That what happens to it is not my choice alone,

That my thoughts must be approved

By the man in my life.

Victimized by the responsibility bestowed upon me

To make amends with the men who have hurt me.

Victimized by the rules of an evolving society

But never a victim.

That would mean defeat.

Pillow Fights, Matches, and Things

Cotton strung around

A ceiling fan.

Halloween on a Tuesday.

Screams from a haunted mind

Reverberate against the walls.

Matches lit vicariously,

Fingers threatening to light more.

Sobs and gobstoppers

Swell into the scene

All beyond control.

Flooding out of me

Until there is nothing left

But dry heaves.

If You Would Just Listen

The first time

I suggested something,

Maybe the anger

Wouldn't swell up

The fumes bubbling to the tip

Of my tongue.

Self-Doubt

His promises seep

Deep into every pore,

Clogging every gap,

Replacing any courage

They tried to hold.

His promises

Leak into the ripples

Of my brain,

Creating new synapses,

Guiding my body toward

Understanding

That she isn't worthy.

Anxiety

He whispers in my ear

Elegant thoughts

Laced with gold and inadequacy.

He taunts me

With my insecurities,

Stitching his words carefully,

Patching my flaws

Onto my psyche

As if I were his model protégé.

I sit on display

For the world to critique.

Who Is That?

But the worst part is that I do not belong

To my own body.

Nothing is attached.

I might just float away

Un-tethered,

Unable to tie down

The emotions ebbing and flowing.

These hands do not belong to me.

That grin in the mirror is not mine.

The tears I've cried,

The moments of pride,

Swell up inside,

Unable to be contained.

Am I going insane?

Fear

Haunting me,

Whispering in my mind

Your treasonous voice

Sifts through bittersweet memories.

All the ifs and possibilities,

The ways danger could have slipped

Into daily routines.

Just walk away from the thoughts,

My conscious mind pleads.

But I am left holding my breath,

Hoping to breathe.

Plugging my ears,

Holding my eyes shut

It's still fear

Slipping into my mouth.

Lapping her up,

Unaware of how to get her

Salty, sticky taffy

Off my tongue.

They'll Ask Me

They'll ask me:

What was I wearing?

They'll ask me:

What was I doing?

Having the audacity

To sway my hips

In their natural way.

To wear clothing

That is form-fitting

And comfortable.

They'll ask me:

What was I thinking?

Going into the night,

Knowing the Moon

Can't bathe me in

Safety.

Daylight

Assault

Happens

In the

Sunlight

In front of

Curious eyes.

Hold On

And when

There's nothing left

Of me,

I will still say:

I love you.

He Loves Me

Do the rules change

When you rest

Your heart

In the hands,

In the carcass of weeds?

He loves me,

He loves me not.

He loves me,

He loves me not.

He loves me,

He loves me not.

He loves me.

He loves me—

Not.

Elektra

Tender, calloused skin

Creates a map around me,

Finding your way to the very beginning

To where

Our bodies once

Belonged to one another.

Basking in your arms:

My protector,

My lover,

My sanctuary.

Mouth Stuff

Filling the time,

Filling my mind

With ways to distract myself

From the heartache of every day.

An obstacle course

Set out before me,

Mulling over anything I can get my hands on:

Gum, crackers, grapes

Or your favorite: cherries

Just to keep my thoughts from wandering.

You often mistake this

For lust,

A craving for your salty skin.

Id

Whisk me away

Into a forest,

Crippled with fireflies,

Fairies, and immortality

Where our love

Can linger.

Let me stretch my body

Beneath yours

And play with the breath

You so willingly share.

Inspire me to dance for you,

Animalistic and sincere.

I cannot wait a second longer.

Ego

My thoughts and ideas

Swirl around the room,

Looking for a place to land.

Weathered into a cheap patina,

They scatter,

Only to find a home

In your barbed-wire notebook

The one you used to betray me.

Still, I let them flow from me,

Dizzy with hope,

Believing you understood

What ailed me.

In Those Eyes

What do you see

When you ask me to

Lie down?

What are you hiding from me

By refusing to look me in the eye?

I want to know you,

Just as you have grown to know me,

Lusting for the moment

Your curtains

Are pulled back,

And we no longer

Twirl around

A false sense of innocence.

Ideation

It was the idea

Of you

That I fell in love with.

It was the idea

That you could listen,

That you could understand.

But reality

Had such a bitter bite.

Your intellect ripped my skin ragged,

Exposing the monsters within,

All for a taste

Of your serpentine lips.

And still,

I'd do it all over again.

Transference

I may not love you

The way you thought I would.

I don't cling to your theories

Like they do in the gentlemen's club.

But I see the thoughts

Spreading inside your soul,

The curiosity

Swimming in your

Penetrating eyes.

When your heart aches,

I am the pill to ease your pain.

My hand will never quiver,

Even when your observations

Lash me.

Dreams

Pretty little nightmare,

I dare you to shimmy closer.

I can feel your winter

Drifting up my spine,

A memory mangling my mind

Worse than the razor to my thighs.

Because,

You, my dear interpreter,

Are my personal monster,

Hiding in the shadows of every dream.

Waiting for me to associate

Every monster

With the one

Who analyzes me.

Ignorance: What Do Women Want?

I grow invisible

In the shadows of your interests,

Gliding between

Your primal desires

And waking wants.

My intentions are lost

Within the maze

You so cleverly built.

Stepping lightly,

Deeper and deeper,

Hoping to catch a glimpse,

Hoping for a chance

To catch your gaze

And tell you

What I truly want.

But we all know

There is no escape.

And that moment

Will never come.

Primal

I want to know

You can feel my fingernails

Deep in the marrow of your bones.

I want your dreams,

Plucked from your pretty head

And laid out before me,

Like a feline displaying her prey.

No Control

The scent of your soul

Drives me wild.

I prowl,

Searching,

Hunting for you,

Yearning for the day

I can sit

And hold my personal

Communion with your flesh and blood.

Pages

You read my pages

As if they were bound

Perfectly in a book,

Reading between the lines,

Creating theories and analyses

From lies

I haven't even written yet.

Hear Me Roar

We march,

And we riot,

Screaming at the top of our lungs.

Still,

Our voices aren't heard.

We don't want a penis

Swinging between our legs.

As if a dick

Contains a brain.

We want the power

That comes with

Such a small and fragile

Organ.

Sensibilities

Undress me

With your interpretations

That swirl in my head

Like poetry.

Let your prose

Turn into

Intimacy surrounding me

With your faraway stare

Helpless

In the love affair.

Paranoia

He can't leave me alone.

Whispers sweet nothings

Into my ears.

He exasperates my fears.

His voice is louder

Than the meds

Louder than your

Untested solutions.

"Help me,"

I begged you.

Words Chosen

You chose your words

By not speaking,

As I associated fictional dreams

With the realities you pretended to hear.

You chose your actions

By not seeking

And discovering the answers

To fix the disconnected lines

Between my psyche

And my biology.

Muddled Crushes

I wanted to taste you,

to lick the caffeine from

your stained teeth

as you thrust yourself

past my innocence.

I wanted to surrender

every fear,

every hope,

every dream

and have you stitch me up

at the seams.

But silence and misunderstanding

were all you offered.

Now these wounds

are gaping and gushing.

Envy

Shattered glass,

maimed by the blood

of broken skin.

Anger sifts from

a metaphor

to the physical world.

Seven years of bad luck

but luck is just a scheme.

Seven years of visits,

of analysis,

and all you could name it

was envy.

The Downfall

The shadows envelop

every inch,

allowing me to slip into

invisibility.

Gliding between desires

and waking wants,

intentions go to waste,

lost in a maze

built without escape.

Mind Games

Thoughts float in a world of their own,

subtly whispering,

subtly drifting out

a tide tied to its moon.

Chemical imbalances

toss thoughts onto the shore

of my unwilling heart

sprayed and weathered,

tugging me closer

to the murky beauty of nothingness.

Understanding the water

creeping up my torso,

I am unable to comprehend,

unable to feel,

the icy betrayal

that is to come.

Tongue Tied

Unsure how to start

This one,

Full of the could-be's,

Would-be's,

I-wish-it-had-be's.

Lifting a heart was nobody's game,

But I wanted to play.

Your poker face

Never gave it away

It also never let me stray

From the path,

Tying my tongue,

Unable to fully express

What is ailing me.

Rest Cure

Take time out of

The juggling acts

You're expected to perform.

Schedule time:

Take a shower, eat a hot meal, sip some coffee.

Self-care is nothing more than basic human dignity.

But

You must still be able to juggle:

The appointments,

Tennis, Girl Scouts, Wrestling, Date Night.

Oh, you also work full time.

Preparing meals, running errands, the toilets don't scrub
themselves.

Doctors still forge empathy,

Prescribe rest

As if we are Perkins Gilman.

Suggesting if we just alienate,

The pressures would melt from

Delicate frames,

As we watch the worlds we've built

Burn away.

Intruding

How much blood

Would splatter

If the railing broke

Beneath my weight?

Who would identify me

If someone ran the red light

And smashed me

Into unrecognizable smithereens?

What would 300 papercuts

Feel like

Simply from flipping through a book?

How much would I feel?

How long would I heal

If I survived at all?

On Edge

Fright never announces

When she walks into a room.

Instead,

She waits until all the breath

Is let out of these lungs.

She becomes a whisper,

A breath fluttering in unsuspecting ears.

She slinks over every inch of skin,

Reminding me

There were days

When my body was not safe.

She glides over good intentions,

Swapping them out for

Misconceptions,

Startling me every time.

Queen of Hearts

Heartstrings,

Pulled into chaos.

Pain inflicts itself

A successful

coup d'état,

Performed effortlessly

On their unsuspecting queen,

Sending her into

Riots within her own

Head.

While the haughty king

Watches ignorantly,

Aware.

Keeping the Keys

Keeping the keys between my fingers,

Knowing exactly where to always hide

The exits, the stairwells, the back doors.

Being ready at a moment's notice:

For when the guy in the green hoodie pulls

A gun on the crowd,

For when a fight breaks out

Between those two girls,

For when the popcorn machine

Explodes,

For when my ex finally finds me

And seeks his revenge,

For when my exiled past comes at me

In a car,

For when the plane loses a vital part

We crash mercilessly To the ground,

For when I misstep and

Fall down the cliff,

For when my child

Doesn't come home.

For when your studies desert me,

And I'm left to my own devices.

Opinion

I never asked you

For permission.

Your opinion

Can't stop me anymore.

Stale

I wanted to force

The will of nature,

Bend it until it broke.

I wanted to

Tear the stigma in half.

I wanted.

I waited.

But you never loved me.

And then I didn't

Want you anymore.

Wildflower

I tried so hard

To be like them,

But my petals didn't blossom

The way theirs did.

My roots grew deeper.

My color grew wild.

Last Year

You betrayed me.

You whispered

Sweet nothings to my soul,

Filled with promises

Of better days,

Promises

Of changing your ways.

Your Cheshire Cat grin

Beguiled and entranced me,

Let me wander through

Your labyrinth.

While I was focused on

Finding your

Intentions,

I found something

Much better instead.

I found

Myself.

I lost the need to impress.

And while I drifted through

The loneliness,

I found a friend

My own spark.

While you were busy suffocating

Us all,

I began to

Breathe.

Because of you,

I know where I am going.

So, thank you

For your cruelty.

Without it,

I'd never know

My true worth.

Eye Contact

How can I trust someone

Who can't even

Look me in the

Eyes?

Do my words even make it

To your ears,

Or do they run away

With your absent stare

Clinging to the walls,

Hanging from the lamps,

Asphyxiating themselves

With the ropes of denial,

And no chair to stand on?

Mommy

Maybe if you just asked your mom

During your weekly

Date,

You could gain some insight

On what it takes

To be a woman

One who constantly

Fawns over

The men in her life.

Road to Understanding

Looking back at all the dreams

I have given you,

Laid them placidly

At your feet

Hoping one day

You would tread on them,

Allowing you

Into my subconscious

Vulnerable, exposed.

And instead, you

Refused to tread upon

The dark velvet pleas,

Afraid to find out

What unfulfilled fantasies I possess.

Misunderstanding

A woman's body

Is filled with secrets.

A woman's body

Doesn't want to hold them.

But it is our job

To keep them

From the limelight.

It's our job

To let your dominance

Overtake us

And still let you call us hysterical

When the secrets become too much,

When the psychological beatings

Begin to crush.

Castrated

Unable to look beyond

Your own biology,

Thinking that

The male body

Is perfectly developed,

You decided

That the lack of a penis

Is what causes my frustration

When in reality,

I couldn't stand

Such a weak and sensitive

Extremity,

Swinging from side to side,

Always reminding me

Of my fragility.

Forbidden Crush

I looked to you

For answers

You couldn't give.

I looked to you

For kisses

You never gifted.

I looked to you

For comfort

That was forbidden.

Floating

You never dared

To dive deeper,

Fully aware,

Fully cognizant

That there was more

To my subconscious.

But even you agreed

The waters surrounding me

Were too murky.

Slip

Slip under my lips

Just this one time.

I heard you when you said

You'd sleep with me,

Despite your claim

That you simply meant

You'd see me again.

Let's Play a Game

Roll the dice

Which dream do we analyze?

The one where I'm trapped,

Running breathless

In a never-ending maze?

The one where my babies die?

Or worse

Betray me to an exiled life?

Or do we dare to wander

Where the world turns a blind eye,

And I relive every moment

Of my waking life,

Trapped inside a society

That still sees me as something

To be bought,

Something to be possessed?

Violent Creatures

Putting the "y" in why,

Nestled inside your chromosomes,

The need for dominance

Still remains.

Residues of the lie

That we are safe

Calcify

With each

Emotional lashing

We take.

Diamonds Are So Last Decade

Indifference

Is a girl's

Best friend.

She allows us

To courtesy and confess,

Her lure bringing us

To our knees,

Fueling our desire

To hang on to each syllable

Of your demanding drawl,

Forgetting all our wistful

Wishes and wants,

Enabling us

To complete this complicated

Choreography

Inside your head.

Wishful

I wanted so badly

For your assumptions

To be right,

For your answers to hold tight.

You filled me with your

Incantations, assumptions, and potions,

Letting me gulp down every

Accusation.

But the cocaine is wearing off;

The answers are becoming

Unclear.

If only I could suck the ideas

From your lips

Maybe then

We'd find a

Cure.

Experimenting

Lacing our lives together,

You let me lead,

But I never learned

How to dance

In silence.

Backwards and awkward,

You wanted to lean

Into my world,

Just as much as I

Leaned into yours.

Nevertheless,

The idea of our bodies

Intertwining

Became too much to bear.

In unison,

We came

To different realizations

Of what it meant

To explore.

Entice Me

You have noticed

The desires I keep

Tightly between my ribs.

I fear that if not let out soon,

To bask in your daylight,

They may break free

From their fleshy cell,

Leaving my emotions

Splattered across the floors

Of your study

Hurling themselves into a world

Of attention at last.

Drip

So many names

Have been draped across

My back,

Threatening to crush

The strength

They all say I have.

The weight of

Stereotypes

Leaves me waning,

Powerless and defeated,

Until my body

Drips

Into

The soul of

Defeat.

My Love

My love deserves

To expand

Beyond the confines

Of this room.

My passion deserves

To stretch

Beyond your observations

Of what I could be,

Of what I should be,

Of what fucking ideology

You would like to

Slip deliberately

Down my throat.

Inadequate

Inadequacy dances

Around me,

Mocking my trivial pursuit

Of understanding

Myself.

He captures me

In his dizzying dance,

Knowing full well

I don't know the steps

Forcing me to

Follow his lead,

Blindfolded and afraid

That his point will be made.

Focus

I can't

Fucking

Focus.

Knowing that I was built

To fail,

I can't

Focus on anything

When these thoughts

Enrapture me

Reminding my heart

That frailty was built within her,

That she harbors insecurities

No vorpal sword can slay,

That her words will be twisted

And framed

Into a psychological definition.

Piercing Eyes

What are you afraid of

When you avoid my eyes?

Do I scare you?

Maybe.

Maybe all I ever wanted

Was to be given

The same delicacies and luxuries

Like dignity beyond chastity,

Like a voice

To lift up

My dormant dreams.

Jealousy

Jealousy wrapped his

Hands around my neck

Again today.

He thrust his severe

Yearning into the nooks

And crannies of my heart.

I watched

The world move on

Without a single thought,

Leaving me to asphyxiate

On my own unmet

Desires.

Broken Wings

The part that hurt

The most

Was when you turned

Your back,

Afraid to meander

Through my porcelain thoughts

Or play in my

Violet dreams.

My skin grows cold where

Your lingering fingers

Once rested.

Unapologetically,

You left me

To tend

To these broken wings.

Wrung Out

Wringing out my skin,

Looking for every

Last

Drop.

You hung me up to dry

In the frigid sunlight.

My remains

A banner of accomplishment,

A message of deceit,

And unmet desires.

Waving around

For the panel

Of

Intellectuals

To discuss

The meaning of my

Humanity.

Bravery

And she laid there,

Shattered

In your palm,

Silently waiting

For answers,

For tenderness,

For apologies

To glue her back together.

But

You were never

Brave

Enough.

Moments

It's in those moments

Where the sun glints,

Refracting the decency in your eyes,

Perpetuating a sense of beauty and pride.

When the faux warmth

Glances my way,

My heart threatens to explode,

Leaving droplets of my mind

All over your skin

Forgetting that this is

A transactional relationship.

Take Note

Hurriedly,

Your pen scurries across the paper,

Trying to lap up

The indecencies I mutter,

Transcribing and translating

My chaotic storm

Into something

That can be categorized and cataloged.

Yet,

You are unaware of the notes

I am scribbling inside the folds

Of my memory

Of you desperately trying

To understand me.

Observations

You say

It was God's will

To put me on this planet,

Birth your children,

Labor within the home,

And wait for you to come.

You say it was God's will

That I was created weak,

Filled with hysteria,

Sobbing for phallic objects to fill

Unmet needs.

But there was something forgotten,

The sanity I held so close.

Society

His weight shifts

Over me.

His darkness reminds me that I am

Laying frail.

For lack of better words,

Confusion might fit better

Or betrayal.

Betrayal was inevitable,

Unbuttoning my dress,

Taking advantage of the collective strength

In numbers.

Silencing my mouth

As he whispers,

"It's okay, you want this, I promise,"

Stripping away every ounce of decency,

Peeling away the dreams

He ever pretended to give me.

Diagnosed

With your pen,

You lace intricate words

Upon my body

Bright,

Red,

Scarlet letters of possible diagnoses.

They embrace

The freckles on my face,

Embed themselves

In the folds of my skin,

Branding me

With elaborate lettering,

As if the world deserves to put a name

To my afflictions.

As if naming them

Will fix anything

Without understanding why.

These words blaze across my body,

Fueling the fires in my mind.

Not All Men

Not all men

Masquerade the way you do

Masked in petulance,

Dressed and draped in knowledge,

Or at least the idea of it.

Watching quietly

As I swap

Cutting for sex,

Sex for inebriation,

Inebriation for…

All to avoid

The pain

Of Clarity.

Clarity that some men

Have caused me.

And I pretend

That I ever had control.

Because it was never a compliment,

Never my fault.

But still,

I am forced

To live with the guilt of it all.

Panic Attack

The aftershock

Sends these hands into tremors,

And my body knows now

What it must do.

Every cell begins to clamor,

Seeking, searching desperately for

Higher ground.

Filled with unrelenting fear,

Knowing full well

Everything will soon

Be engulfed

A tsunami of heart-breaking

Anger.

I Want

A voice

That is heard and respected.

To allow me to say the things

Without the scrutiny of society.

A say in the way

My body is portrayed,

My life unfolds,

My story is told.

Full autonomy over what

Hobbies fill my days,

The parenting practices I follow,

What I do or don't do with my organs.

To live without the fear of

Being harmed by hands

That are supposed to protect.

The assumption that I am weak

Because of the chromosomes

In my body.

Zombie

Emotions suppressed,

Laid to rest

They are supposed to never die,

So you say.

Yet I am expected to keep

Quiet, demure,

To make you feel much more

Comfortable.

But these feelings,

They fester,

As my skin and body ulcerate.

Fervently, they begin to

Claw their way through my mouth,

Forcing every muscle to

Contort, purge,

Making a fool of myself.

Anatomy

Your idea of destiny

Never meant much to me.

But if you must,

At least

Tell me I'm more than

Pretty.

Silence

The absence

Of

Words

Is often

Louder

Than

Screaming.

Puzzling

Slipping in and out

Of my peripheral vision,

Gliding into the

Fractals

Of my life.

I fill the room with

Sadness-ridden riddles.

You listen

All the same,

Waiting for me

To call your name.

When all I wanted

Grief, angst

Was for you to return the favor.

Instead,

You wait,

Silently rifling through

My sentences,

Refraining from saying

A thing.

Numb

Numbness

Folds herself,

Wrapping her arms around me,

Forcing my thoughts to shed like dead skin.

Emotions peel away

Under her firm grasp,

Leaving only traces of

Her indifferent scent.

Tunnel Vision

Stunned into silence,

Images reflect from the mind's projector,

Showcasing staunch, horrific imagery,

Waiting for me to scream.

But this time,

The words cannot muster themselves

Into developed sounds.

They sit and glisten,

Unable to escape this

Wonka Tunnel from hell.

I can't describe to you what I see

It doesn't make sense.

The haunting images disappear

Before I can even begin to comprehend them.

Swirling

Swirling skies above,

Chants circle dark clouds

Of the could-have-beens,

If only you

Had the courage

To admit

You

Loved me.

Echoes

Climbing through

Dark, cavernous alleys,

You tried

To understand me.

But all you found

Were echoes

Of my screams.

Eggshells

Prickly little things,

Slightly stepping,

Ever so lightly,

Trying not to disturb the peace

Of what my role in society brings.

Allowing myself to feel the sharp pains

With every breath of defiance,

Reminded of my place.

Knowing that eventually,

The weight of my feet

Will tarnish this reputation,

Earning me a soft landing to dance in,

While you're left scratching

At the festering wound of confusion

I've left for you.

Suppressed

Ghastly, appalling, grotesque memories,

Tucked away in the swishes of my dress,

Guiding me along the path

You refuse to see.

Does it hurt to think about the things

I've been through?

Every time I was discounted in your name,

Every time I was belittled and betrayed.

Why should you be more ashamed than the victim?

Is it because you'd have to face the truth?

These memories aren't suppressed;

They were sewn into silence

For the comfort of my observers.

I'm not crazy.

Embrace Me

I want to snuggle

Into the darkness,

Bathe in my own mystery.

At least here,

I can be myself.

At least here,

I can breathe,

Without the fear

Of scrutiny.

Insomniac

Sleep

Has never been good to me

An unhealthy, unreliable codependency.

I need him to live,

I need him to breathe,

But he's never loved me

The way I deserve.

Sleep constantly flaunts

His niceties,

Dangling them as I flail,

Trying to grasp

The morsels my fingers can touch.

And just before I give up,

He grants me peace

Just enough to incite

This dependency,

This addiction.

Only to revoke my privileges,

Binding me to the

Wheels of misfortune,

The spirals

Of sleep deprivation.

The worst part?

Knowing you

Won't save me.

I will

Have to save

Myself.

Mind Trap

Indignant,

Unreasonable, inconsistent

I move from one thought

To the next,

Trying to find

The end of the maze.

But it seems

Destruction

Might just catch up with me.

He has cast his hazy eyes

And will not let me go.

I know this will be lethal.

But whose will

Sends me into decay?

The sickness menacing me

My entire life,

Or my lack of strength,

My inability to find an escape?

No longer able to

Ward off the demons

In my mind.

Neurotypical

Fidgeting constantly

The click of every pen,

Distracting.

The air floating over my skin,

Dismissing any attempt

At a thought process.

I am unable to claw my way

Out of this head fog,

Unable

To fistfight this ideation

That the world is crashing down.

I am unable to

Describe in words

The feelings welling up inside,

Until they break out of this calloused body

Unable to contain

My rebel yell.

Malignant

Malignant thoughts

Blister beneath the skin,

A stark reminder

To my fragile soul

Of what I could become.

Drenched

Drenched in sadness,

I wade through turbulent waters.

Betrayal lines her currents,

And I find myself waiting

Waiting to emerge

From her riptide.

Framed

Somewhere in the in-between,

Your lies faded.

Somewhere in the in-between,

My mind grew faint,

And they blurred,

Blending into an eternal frame

Where I am bound to keep

My pain,

My muse,

My entire existence.

Pick Me

I crave the attention.

The tension

It's too much.

Snooping

Drifting through

your papers,

lost in a cold frenzy,

I realized

everything between us

was transactional.

Small

You made me

lie down,

shrink myself smaller,

just so you could

tower

over what ailed me,

pretending to be

some sort of hero.

But not even your

peers took you

seriously.

Stripped

Layer by layer,

your delicate hands

stripped away

the labels

and assumptions

until you reached

what was thought

to be my core.

You bound me tightly

towards intimacy,

believing you'd

finally glimpsed

my innermost thoughts.

Rose Petals

Softly,

the petals of my thoughts

fall into the laps

of your peers.

They meander

in the staleness

of their stares.

Mirrors

If I could find the switch

to turn the light on,

maybe

you'd see beyond the man

staring back at you

and glimpse the shadows

of what is really happening

inside my mind.

Maybe

if you scratched at the

silver surface,

you'd peep

into the psyche of a woman.

Maybe

you're too afraid,

so, you simply

blame my hormones

for your lack

of consideration.

Just a Thought

Maybe we should test women

For the products

We prescribe them.

See how their bodies

Interact

Instead of male mice.

Maybe fewer of us

Would die.

D.D.

Anger

It begins to bubble and bob

Between each vein,

Shredding any decency

And reminders to behave.

She shells out one bullet,

Then two, then three

From my mouth

Unable to hold my tongue,

For fear it too will fall out.

Anger nestles

Into the nucleus of my cells,

Unable to be controlled,

Unable to be quelled.

Ice Queen

How can you demand

Empathy,

Understanding,

Submission,

When there is nothing left

Of me to give?

Control Me

Back against the wall,

Heavy breathing,

The heat of your mouth

Lingering on my neck.

Your soft power

Drifts

Over every inch

Of my body.

Knowing

I am exactly

Where you want me,

I lean in.

You know you want

To fuck me.

Manic

A whirlwind

in the mind,

taking up

all blank spaces.

Eloquently,

around hopes and dreams,

blotting passion-filled

ink

all over my aspirations.

Stringing words and phrases,

allowing these eyes to see

all the beauty life can be.

Pretending

Tiptoeing

around the edges

of insanity

the dance I've always known.

Fluttering from

group to group,

sipping the tea,

pretending to have just an ounce

of normalcy.

Thunder on a Sunny Day

When the thunderclouds

roll into my skies,

the warmth of the sun

drifts away,

unable

to save me.

Madame Madness

Her dark cloud

drifts over me

unannounced,

uninvited.

I can't stop her.

She lurks on my skin

until I allow her

to slip inside.

She halts my spirit,

lacking any sense of remorse.

And when she's had her fill of me,

she leaves,

as if nothing ever happened.

Death

She throws pebbles

at our windows.

She serenades

every wish and desire.

Still,

we must look away.

She breaks into our homes,

whispering,

"It's time."

She follows us

from room to room,

waiting for the moment

we surrender.

She waits

for when we decide to part ways

with breath

and blindly follow her

to her vacant forever.

Found

Clutching a key

With intent,

Fascinated by

Success,

Opportunities,

I

Was

Ready

To

Leave.

Crocodile Tears

Tears well uncontrollably,

Unable to be stopped,

Unable to be detected.

The instant earthquake beneath my lids

They just

Gush, gush, gush.

And that's when I realize

That even the pain

From a sudden

Drop,

From a sudden

Slip,

A sudden

Mistake,

Intentional or not,

Would be welcomed over

The numbness that makes me question

Whether or not I'm alive.

Womanhood

He sat there,

Blaming my emotions

On the monthly

Ritual

Surrounding the mistress moon

My kindred heart

As my world

Shatters,

Falls,

Slowly

Apart.

Minor Disturbance

Clarity

Dissolves

Pixie dust

Falling between

Tinkerbell's spiteful fingers,

Descending into

Another bit

Of

Chaos.

Say Something

Words sit,

Scrambled and cold,

Waiting for validation

To strike.

Hungry for something to say,

Starving to be taken seriously.

Unavailable

Sullen answers for

Unasked questions,

Leading me astray

From the path

Of coherent thought.

Holding my hand,

Refusing to let go,

She reminds me

There is no way out.

Transported

It is his hands

That glide over my thigh

In the thick of the night

His lips that touch mine.

My heart quickens,

My skin thickens,

And I am falling

Into the dark space,

Into the place where

My mind

Can dissociate.

Blurred Lines

Heavy breathing,

Heart pounding,

Images seared into my mind.

Images that cannot be shaken

From memory.

As my feet finally touch the ground,

Out of the comfort of my bed,

Trauma pulses through my veins.

Unable to decide

If the crying, the screaming, the bloodshed,

The constant fear,

Were just a dream,

You assured me.

Grief

Her dense fog

Drenches me,

Soliciting illicit thoughts

Of what could have been.

Covering the sunlight,

Denying warmth,

Leaving me

Unable to move,

Unable to speak.

With my best interest

In mind,

The blankets of submission

Were draped

Sweetly,

Eloquently,

Around my shoulders

Eliminating

Every inch I had to stand on.

Quietly,

Silencing my voice.

Gently,

Taking away my strength.

Hypothesis

Slowly,

I picked up the

Fragments

Of my mind

And placed

Them delicately

On the shelf.

Arranging them

Into something much

Stronger

Than your

Hypotheses.

Crumbs

There are only

So many ways

A soul can

Crumble

Before it's too late.

Reality

There is no grip to get,

There is no hand to squeeze,

No rules to tease.

There is nobody

Who will truly listen.

But I promise you

This isn't hysteria.

This isn't a hormonal

Imbalance.

It's the teetering of a human

Soul, bargaining with the devil,

Hoping to crash into the depths of the sea

Just for a little relief from the systems

We are forced to feed from,

From the diagnostics

That don't seek reason.

This is the sound of a heart

After it has shattered

Into the finest sand,

Knowing that the breeze

Will likely spread

The pieces like ashes

A flame extinguished

Before the wax ever ran out.

Disturbed

Disturbed is a word

For the bourgeoisie,

For the misunderstood,

Wanting the world

To think there is an answer.

But really,

The symptoms

Still mystify

And brilliantly defy

The status quo.

Gardens

How many flowers

Have been plucked

From naïve gardens,

Then taunted

For their unkempt

Purity.

Dumb Belles

A woman's strength

Is only measured

By

The burdens

She can carry,

And still

Maintain a smile.

Sweat

Frigid air,

Sweaty palms,

Sweaty back

Sweat sweetly slips

Between furrowed brows,

Unable to be stopped.

Washing away

Any sense of clarity,

Exposed,

Rinsed clean.

A naked rat

Is what is left of me.

Blurred Lines

Heavy breathing,

Heart pounding,

Images seared into my mind

Images that cannot be shaken

From memory.

As my feet

Finally touch the ground,

Out of the comfort of my bed,

Trauma pulses through my veins.

Unable to decide

If the crying,

The screaming,

The bloodshed,

The constant fear

Was just a dream.

You assured me.

Transported

It is his hands

That glide over my thigh

In the thick of the night.

His lips touch mine,

My heart quickens,

My skin thickens.

And I am falling

Into the dark space,

Into the place

Where my mind

Can dissociate.

The Only Trope We Belong To

And then

She

Let out

The breath

She didn't even know

She was holding.

Insecurity

Taking the time

To meticulously erase

Every line,

Every trace,

Every ounce of dirt

That could hang from

The convictions

Rummaging within my brain.

Womanhood

He sat there,

Blaming my emotions

On the monthly ritual

Surrounding the mistress moon—

My kindred heart—

As my world shatters,

Falls,

Slowly apart.

When a 28-day cycle

Is broken down,

You're never too far

From the start.

Drowning

Drowning is lonely

When it happens within the crumples

Of a brain,

Fighting upstream

To catch

A breath,

A break,

A moment of solace.

Sunshine and Butterflies

Sunrises burst across my face,

Leaving me floating

Above a bed of wildflowers,

Soaring high,

Smiling wide.

Knowing this won't last,

I suck in every sweet breath,

Clinging to every heartbeat,

Every piece of laughter,

Because this feeling

Is sure to surrender.

A Dying Dream

Creativity dangles

Helplessly,

Motionless,

Breathless

While biased observations,

Calloused ideations,

Are the

Rope

Around

My neck.

Monster

Because of you,

I'm no longer

Afraid

Of monsters.

A. Skoda boasts professional experience in everything from technical writing, novel writing, and poetry. In 2024, she received her MA of Fine Arts with a concentration in English studies through ASU. Since she was in her teens, she has closely studied psychology largely focusing on Sigmund Freud and Carl Jung's approaches to the field. Skoda uses her writing to connect her love of literature and psychology.

www.ingramcontent.com/pod-product-compliance
Lightning Source LLC
Chambersburg PA
CBHW021138130626
46554CB00005B/1567